BRAVO! 6

Activity Book

Judy West

MACMILLAN HEINEMANN
English Language Teaching

Lesson 1

A Choose, complete and say

to until about of after ~~for~~

Jane Hello, Bill. How are you?

Bill Fine, thanks. What are you doing?

Jane We're doing our radio programme.

Bill What do you mean?

Anna We're making radio programmes ..for.. the school.
Our first programme is .... languages.
Why don't you help us?

Bill That's a good idea. What about Hiro, Jack and Lisa?

Anna They can help too. It'll be a lot .... work. But we can use the library .... school.

Bill Great. I'll help you.

Anna Good. We can go .... the library now. It'll be open .... five o'clock.

Look and write

Look at Nadia and David's timetable.

	Monday	Tuesday	Wednesday	Thursday	Friday
1	English	Geography	History	Science	English
2	Art	Maths	English	Art	Library
			B R E A K		
3	Maths	Science	Maths	Maths	Music
			L U N C H		
4	Science	Library	History	Geography	Maths
5	Science	Music	Sports	Sports	History

1 How many English lessons do they have every week? *They have three English lessons every week.*

2 How many maths lessons do they have? ....

3 Which subject do they have first on Tuesdays?

....

4 Which subject do they have last on Fridays?

....

5 Which subject do they have after break on Wednesdays?

....

6 Which subject do they have before lunch on Mondays?

....

B Answer

Write your answers and your friend's answers.

1 What is your favourite subject at school?

....

2 How many English lessons do you have each week?

....

3 How many maths lessons do you have each week?

....

4 How long are your lessons?

....

5 What is your English teacher's name?

....

6 How many pupils are there in your class?

....

7 Where do you have your English lessons?

....

8 Do you like learning English?

....

C Complete

1	.........Can we......... use the library after school?	Yes, of course you can.
2	.... interested in music?	Yes, I am.
3	.... don't we do a programme about pets?	That's a good idea.
4	.... will the programmes be?	They'll be one hour long.
5	.... is the library?	It's next to our classroom.
6	.... knows a lot about sports?	I do.
7	.... think it's a good idea?	Yes, I do.

Lesson 2

A Choose and complete

because so and

1 Carlos is crying ....so......... his mother will pick him up.

2 I'm learning English .... I want to go to the United States.

3 I like English very much .... I like Spanish, too.

4 Most children can say about twenty words .... understand more than two hundred before they are eighteen months old.

5 He's learning English .... his grandfather lives in California.

6 Millions of children speak one language at home .... learn a different language at school.

7 I'm going to the library .... I need a book for my homework.

8 Babies listen .... slowly learn to speak.

9 Many people learn English .... it is very useful.

10 I want to be a doctor .... I must learn English.

Answer

Why are you learning English? ....

....

....

B Complete

Japan	....Japanese....	....	Chinese
Spain	....	Portugal	....
France	....	Thailand	....
....	Korean	Greece	....
Italy	....		

Find out

Which languages do people speak in these countries?

Argentina Mexico Brazil The United States Malaysia Egypt

Write

Add capital letters and full stops (.) or question marks (?) to these sentences.

1 in english, the alphabet has twenty-six letters

In English, the alphabet has twenty-six letters.

2 other languages use different alphabets

....

3 it is very difficult to learn chinese

....

4 when are you going to japan

....

5 do you prefer maths or english

....

C Look and write

Look at the graph of children's first languages in this school.

True or false? T/F

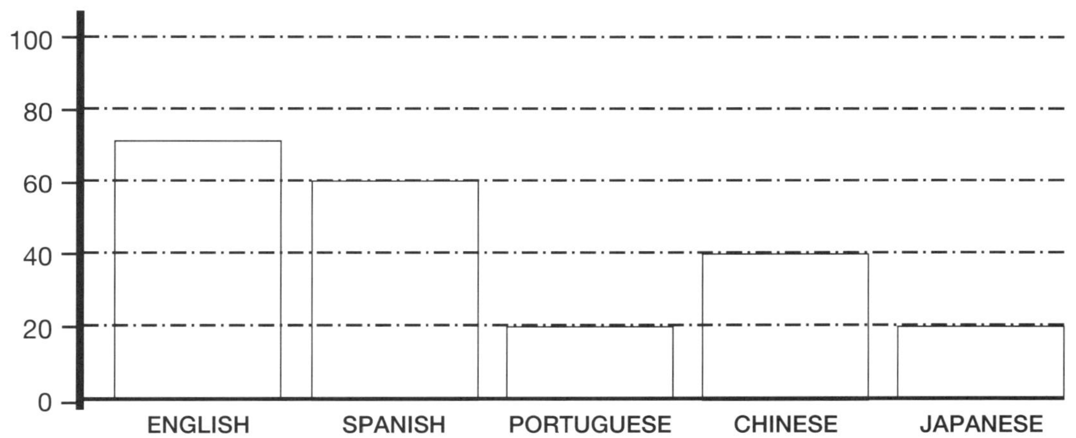

1 More than half the children speak English as a first language. ☐

2 More children speak Spanish than Portuguese. ☐

3 Less than half the children speak Chinese. ☐

4 More than fifty children speak Japanese. ☐

5 There are more than two hundred children in the school. ☐

6 More children speak English than Spanish. ☐

7 More children speak Chinese than Japanese. ☐

Lesson 3

A Read and complete

Read this conversation.
Then write down Juan's answers to the questionnaire.

Lisa What is your first language, Juan?
Juan Spanish.
Lisa And your second language?
Juan English, of course. I started learning it when I was six.
Lisa Does everyone in your family speak English?
Juan My parents speak it a little. But my brother isn't very good at English.
Lisa Can you read English easily?
Juan Yes, I can read newspapers and short books easily. But I can't read very difficult books.
Lisa Can you write in English?
Juan Yes, I can, but not very well. I write to my American pen pal in English.
Lisa Do you know any songs in English?
Juan Yes, I love English songs. I never sing in Spanish.
Lisa Do you know any other language?
Juan No, I don't. I tried to learn German but it was too difficult.
Lisa Thanks very much, Juan.

Q. 1 What is your first language? **A.** ....
Q. 2 What is your second language? **A.** ....
Q. 3 Does everyone in your family speak your second language? **A.** ....
Q. 4 Have you ever read a book in this language? **A.** ....
Q. 5 Have you ever written a letter in this language? **A.** ....
Q. 6 Do you know any songs in the language? **A.** ....
Q. 7 Have you ever learnt another language? **A.** ....

Now ask your friend the same questions.
Write down your friend's answers to the questionnaire.

1 ....
2 ....
3 ....
4 ....
5 ....
6 ....
7 ....

Answer

Yes, I have/No, I haven't.

1 Have you ever been to Hong Kong? ....
2 Have you ever eaten octopus? ....
3 Have you ever seen a UFO? ....
4 Have you ever studied Japanese? ....
5 Have you ever been in an aeroplane? ....

B Listen, look and write

Which object is each person talking about?
Write the correct number next to each object.

C Choose and write

Write the words from the box below in the correct lists.

history	geography	tennis	science	football	physics	maths	swimming
	biology	volleyball	basketball	English	skiing	baseball	

	School subjects	Sports
1	history .... ☐	.... ☐
2	.... ☐	.... ☐
3	.... ☐	.... ☐
4	.... ☐	.... ☐
5	.... ☐	.... ☐
6	.... ☐	.... ☐
7	.... ☐	.... ☐

Tick the subjects you do. Tick the sports you do.

Lesson 4

A Choose and complete

with	about	to	at	in

Come ...to... the school video club! This week we are showing a video .... life .... Japan. It is called *East meets West.* Come .... the School Hall .... 4.30 pm. After the video there will be a free glass of orange juice .... the Dining Room. Come .... your friends!

B Complete

January
F...ebruary...
M...
A...
M...
J...
J...
A...
S...
O...
N...
D...

Monday
T...uesday...
W...
T...
F...
S...
S...

Look and write

Write the time under each clock.

four o' clock ....

....

Look and write

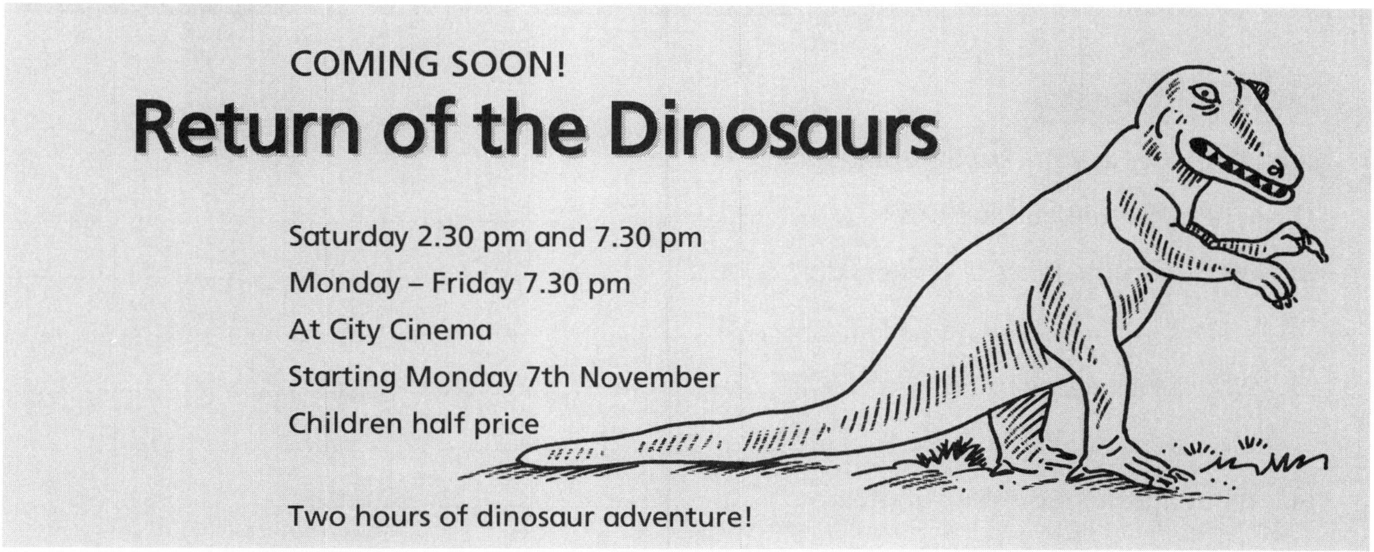

1 Is *Return of the Dinosaurs* a film or a play? It's a film.

2 Which day will it start? ....

3 Can you see it on Sundays? ....

4 Will there be half price seats for children? ....

5 What time will it start on Wednesdays? ....

....

6 What time will it finish on Saturday afternoon? ....

....

C Read and circle

Circle the words with similar meanings.

little fat sorry happy small tall

pleased angry quick delighted silly amazing

talk laugh run decide speak come

language lesson teacher class letter address

correct clever happy difficult right long

begin song language date start

Lesson 5

A Read and answer

Read the story in your Pupil's Book again.

1 Where did the animals live? ....

2 Why were the lakes and rivers dry? ....

....

3 Where was the wishing tree? ....

....

4 What did the mountain goat know? ....

....

5 Which animal could run very fast? ....

6 Did the mountain goat say the name of the wishing tree? ....

7 Did the tiger remember the name? ....

8 Who went up the mountain next? ....

....

9 What was the bull thinking while it was running down the mountain? ....

....

10 Why did the animals laugh at the tortoise? ....

....

B Read, choose and complete

proudly	quickly	carefully	quietly	slowly

The animals wanted someone to run ....quickly.... up the mountain. They needed to know the name of the wishing tree because they were thirsty and the wishing tree could give them one wish. The mountain goat knew the name of the tree. It said the name very .... to the tiger. The tiger repeated the name .... The tiger ran down the mountain but it couldn't remember the name. Then the bull ran up the mountain to find out the name but it couldn't remember it either. So the tortoise walked .... up the mountain and down again. It stood in front of the tree and called out ...., 'Uvuganlma.'

Complete

1 A Did he learn Chinese quickly?

B Yes, he learnt Chinese very quickly.

2 A Can an ostrich run fast?

B Yes, it can run very fast.

3 A Does a parrot sing loudly?

B Yes, ...

4 A Does a snail move slowly?

B Yes, ...

5 A Does an owl fly quietly at night?

B Yes, ...

C Look and match

Number each picture correctly.

1 A long time ago, some animals decided to have a race.

2 'Who can win a race to the forest?' said the deer.

'I can,' said the hare. 'I can run very fast.'

3 'I can win the race,' said the tortoise. The animals laughed.

'Let me try before you laugh at me,' said the tortoise.

4 The hare and the tortoise started together.

5 But the hare stopped because the tortoise was very slow. He went to sleep under a tree.

6 So the tortoise finished first.

'I am slow,' he said, 'but I didn't go to sleep.' The hare was very angry.

Lesson 6

A Listen and circle

Circle the sentence you hear.

1 Can we use them after school?

Can we use it after school?

2 What are we going to do?

What are they going to do?

3 Why do you want to invite him to the party?

Why do you want to invite her to the party?

4 I'm interested in history.

I'm not interested in history.

5 He said we need to learn English.

He said they don't need to learn English.

B Listen, complete and act out

Complete the conversation. Then act it out.

Jim Hello, Jo. How are you?

Jo ....

Jim Where are you going?

Jo ....

Jim You're too late, Jo.

Jo ....

Jim The library closes at 4.00 on Tuesdays.

Jo ....

Jim Why don't we play tennis instead?

Jo ....

C Look, listen and decide

Listen to the cassette. Write A if the sentence is about picture A. Write B if it is about picture B. Write A/B if it is about pictures A and B.

1 .... 2 .... 3 .... 4 .... 5 .... 6 .... 7 .... 8 .... 9 .... 10 ....

Write three questions about the pictures. Ask your friend these questions.

1 ....

2 ....

3 ....

Write your friend's answers.

1 ....

2 ....

3 ....

Lesson 7

A Choose and complete

1 I have five English lessons ....every.... week.

A) every B) ever C) very D) usually

2 It .... very cold in our classroom.

A) were B) are C) can D) was

3 Can I have a sandwich? I'm very ....

A) hungry B) angry C) difficult D) interested

4 Chinese is probably the .... language in the world.

A) more difficult B) difficult C) most difficult D) difficulty

5 There are .... than three hundred children in our school.

A) more B) most C) lots of D) the most

6 I speak two languages. Spanish is my first language and English is my .... language.

A) third B) twice C) new D) second

B Think and decide

It is often busy but there isn't any noise.
It has lots of books but it isn't clever.
The books are often expensive but you don't pay.
What is it?

C Write the questions

1 Fine, thanks.

How are you?..

2 History is my favourite subject.

....

3 No, we don't need our books.

....

4 My first language is French.

....

Lesson 8

A Match

colt		where people keep animals
bucket	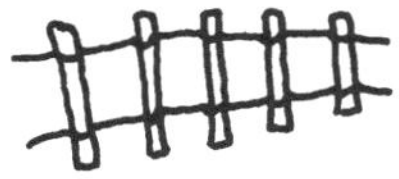	a young horse
stomach		for carrying milk or water
breakfast		goes around a house or a field
farm		part of the body, the middle
fence		first meal of the day

Read and answer

Read the story in your Pupil's Book again.

1 What is Nellie? ....

2 Where does Jody live? ....

3 How old is he? ....

4 Who is Billy Buck? ....

5 Why was Jody's mother pouring hot water into a bucket? ....

....

6 Why must Jody look after Nellie? ....

....

7 Is Jody pleased that Nellie is going to have a colt? ....

8 Why does Billy say he sometimes thinks he is a horse? ....

....

9 Does the horse like Billy? How do you know? ....

....

10 When is Nellie going to have her colt? ....

....

B Write

Write the sentences with the verb in the past.

1 She (is) pouring water. ....She was pouring water.........

2 It (is) a sunny morning. ....

3 Jody (takes) the bucket and (goes) outside. ....

....

4 Nellie (eats) the food and (pushes) the bucket with her nose.

....

5 She (rubs) her head against Jody's arm. ....

....

6 Billy Buck (comes) to talk to Jody. ....

7 Billy (counts) on his fingers. ....

8 Billy (laughs). ....

9 My father (is) old. ....

10 He (looks) at Nellie and (speaks) to her. ....

....

11 Nellie (turns) her head and (looks) into Billy's eyes.

....

C Complete

head	nose	arm	stomach	finger	eyes	hand	mouth	leg	foot	toe

Lesson 9

A Write the questions and discuss

1 Lots of children are interested in television.

Are lots of children interested in television? ....

2 Computers are useful.

....

3 Television is important.

....

4 Computers are difficult to use.

....

5 Homework is important.

....

6 Computer games are interesting.

....

Answer

1 When did you go to Paris? (two months ago) I went to Paris two months ago.

2 When did he get his computer? (six weeks ago) ....

....

3 When did you learn to type? (a year ago) ....

....

4 When did you start English lessons? (a month ago) ....

....

5 When did you lose your passport? (six months ago) ....

....

6 When did we do the spelling test? (three days ago) ....

....

B Choose and complete

~~write~~ win drive visit fly

1 One day I might ....write.......... a book.

2 When I'm twenty-five I might .... Australia.

3 One day I might .... a big car.

4 One day you might .... a competition.

5 One day we might .... to the moon.

C Look and write

1 Sam likes history.

One day ....he might be an archaeologist.....

....

2 Sally is interested in first aid.

One day ....

....

3 Steve likes keep fit exercises.

One day ....

....

4 Harry likes trains.

One day ....

....

5 Alice is interested in animals.

One day ....

....

6 Josh likes school exams!

One day ....

....

doctor head teacher gymnastics teacher archaeologist train driver zoo-keeper

Lesson 10

A Write

1 Have you seen our new computer?

A) No, I haven't seen it yet. B) Yes, I've seen it already.

2 Have you done your maths homework yet?

A) No, ... B) Yes, ...

3 Have you written your essay yet?

A) No, ... B) Yes, ...

4 Have you learnt your spellings yet?

A) No, ... B) Yes, ...

5 Have you started Spanish lessons yet?

A) No, ... B) Yes, ...

6 Have you finished your project yet?

A) No, ... B) Yes, ...

Look and write

1 Has he done his work yet?

No, he hasn't.

2 Has she seen the teacher yet?

....

3 Has she bought a bicycle yet?

....

4 Has he brought his money?

....

B Write

Add capital letters and full stops (.) to these sentences.

1 libraries, shops and offices all use computers

Libraries, shops and offices all use computers.

2 many computers are made in japan and korea

....

3 millions of people around the world have their own computers

....

4 most of the information on computers is in english

....

C Find and say

Can you find thirty English words in this word square? Ask a friend questions.

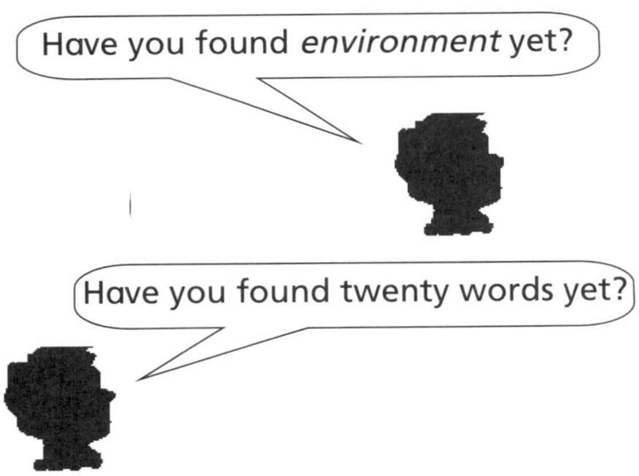

L	C	K	T	M	S	U	B	J	E	C	T	E	S	D	C
A	H	W	R	L	E	T	M	I	N	T	B	C	T	O	O
N	I	P	E	O	P	L	E	B	V	I	D	B	E	L	M
G	N	E	E	M	O	D	U	C	I	O	S	K	L	P	P
U	E	S	T	O	R	E	O	R	R	E	A	D	E	H	U
A	S	J	F	D	R	A	D	I	O	P	D	M	V	I	T
G	E	C	H	I	L	D	R	E	N	L	X	A	I	N	E
E	N	G	L	I	S	H	X	K	M	J	H	G	S	M	R
F	R	E	N	C	H	K	B	P	E	I	K	A	I	N	G
E	G	T	A	H	O	R	S	E	N	U	E	Z	O	S	H
R	L	X	Y	O	Y	E	Z	D	T	L	A	I	N	E	P
F	I	L	M	M	I	B	H	L	E	B	R	N	B	V	D
A	B	K	I	E	T	O	R	T	O	I	S	E	O	I	I
E	R	G	S	W	X	O	B	A	J	F	C	F	C	D	S
N	A	C	L	O	D	K	N	X	W	C	H	T	B	E	C
P	R	O	G	R	A	M	M	V	X	P	O	G	A	O	U
G	Y	P	B	K	S	U	L	G	S	P	O	R	T	S	S
A	D	M	O	U	N	T	A	I	N	M	L	D	R	E	S

Choose and complete

too much enough

1 He watches four hours of television a day. His father says he watches too much television.

2 He didn't pass his exams at school because he didn't do .... homework.

3 Please bring me some milk. I haven't got .... milk here.

4 I can't finish my project today. There is .... to do.

Lesson 11

A Look and write

1 Which thing is the most expensive?

The video camera is the most expensive. ....

2 Which thing is the cheapest?

....

3 Which thing is more expensive than the video but less expensive than the video camera?

....

4 Which thing is more expensive than the calculator but less expensive than the camera?

....

5 Is the radio less expensive than the camera?

....

6 Is the video more expensive than the television?

....

7 Which thing would you like to buy? Say why.

....

B Write and say

£ = pounds

1 £22.50 *Twenty-two pounds fifty.* ....

2 £40 ....

3 £77.50 ....

4 £90.75 ....

5 £4.50 ....

6 £19.40 ....

7 £3.50 ....

8 £4.49 ....

C Choose, complete and say

so	then	too	Would	any	until	called

Bob Hi, Eddie. Where were you last night?

Eddie Hello, Bob. I was very tired. The bus was late .....so........ I didn't get home .... six o'clock.

Bob Did you have .... homework?

Eddie Yes, lots. Maths, science and geography. I finished my geography project. Anyway, I was .... tired to play basketball.

Bob Did you work all evening?

Eddie Well, no. I finished my work at eight o'clock and .... I watched a video with my brother.

Bob What was it?

Eddie Oh, it was very interesting. It was a wildlife video. It was all about penguins. Did you know that some penguins are only forty centimetres tall? .... you like to borrow it?

Bob Thanks. I'd like to. I have a new video. It's a cartoon .... Dangerbirds.

Answer

1 Do you watch television in the morning? ....

2 Do you watch television in the evening? ....

3 How many programmes do you usually watch? ....

4 What is your favourite programme? ....

5 How many hours of television do you watch every week? ....

6 Do your parents say you watch too much television? ....

Now ask a friend these questions. Write about your friend.

1 ....

2 ....

3 ....

4 ....

5 ....

6 ....

Lesson 12

A Decide and write

Make six sentences.

I think /I don't think ...

... hamburgers are delicious.

... pop music is great.

... contests are fun.

... cartoons are silly.

... maths is easy.

... English is difficult.

1 ....

2 ....

3 ....

4 ....

5 ....

6 ....

B Read, choose and complete

collect build look for arrive enjoy learn series

This is a ...series......... of six programmes. The programmes are about three children on a beautiful island. They .... there after a terrible storm. They have no food and nothing to drink. They .... food in the forest. They find bananas and lots of delicious fruit. They .... water and keep it in cups made of banana leaves. They .... a house and they .... to catch fish. They .... swimming in the warm sea and eating the delicious fruit, but one day something happens. Suddenly the children want to leave their beautiful new home.

Choose and complete

this these

1 ...This...... tea is cold. I don't like it.

2 Look at .... tyres. They are very old.

3 .... sheets of paper are too small. I need bigger ones.

4 .... bicycle is too big. I need a smaller one.

C Write

1 Where do they live?

He asked ......where they lived...

2 What do they eat?

She asked ....

3 What do they find?

She asked ....

4 How do they build a house?

He asked ....

5 Why do they make cups out of banana leaves?

She asked ....

6 What do they enjoy doing?

He asked ....

Match

Match the words with their opposites.

1	rich	small
2	expensive	happy
3	silly	cheap
4	fat	worst
5	big	boring
6	best	sensible
7	unhappy	thin
8	exciting	poor

Lesson 13

A Read and answer

Read the story in your Pupil's Book again.

1 Was the computer old? ....

2 Did Carl know how to use the mouse? ....

3 Did Shona know how to use the mouse? ....

4 What happened when Carl moved the mouse? ....

....

5 Whose name did Carl type first? ....

6 Whose name did he type next? ....

7 Why was Shona angry? ....

....

8 How did Carl help Shona? ....

9 Was Carl patient? ....

10 What did Shona type? ....

B Write

Put the verb in the past tense.

1 Shona ....looked.... at the screen and the keyboard but she did not understand anything. (look)

2 Carl .... the computer on. He .... a word. (turn, type)

3 Shona .... letters and numbers on the computer screen. (see)

4 She .... at the computer screen and .... her name. (look, see)

5 She .... but she .... the wrong keys. (try, press)

6 Shona .... to do it, but she .... (want, can't)

7 He .... the pencil to her right hand. (tie)

8 Then she .... the pencil and .... an 'S'. (move, type)

C Look, say and write

Look at the pictures and tell the story, using the words below.

1

2

3

4

5

6

Last week ....

....

....

....

....

....

....

....

bought	turned on	typed	got up	tripped over	lost

Lesson 14

A Listen and circle

Circle the sentence you hear.

1 It's at eight fifteen tonight.
   It's at eight thirty tonight.
2 It's on Thursday at nine thirty.
   It's on Tuesday at nine thirty.
3 It's at seven o'clock on Wednesday morning.
   It's at seven o'clock on Monday morning.
4 He asked me which video I liked.
   He asked me which review I liked.
5 It's too expensive.
   It isn't too expensive.
6 This one's cheaper.
   This one's the cheapest.

B Listen and complete

television calculator camera radio computer

1 I don't have a ...calculator...
2 I always listen to the .... in the mornings.
3 I have already learnt to type on a ....
4 My brother watches too much ....
5 Have you seen my new ....?

C Listen and complete

Listen to Hiro interviewing Angie for the school questionnaire and fill in her answers.

Q. 1 What is your favourite television programme? **A.** ....

....

Q. 2 What other programmes do you watch every week? **A.** ....

....

Q. 3 How many hours of television do you watch every week? **A.** ....

....

Q. 4 Do you watch television before you do your homework? **A.** ....

....

Q. 5 Do you watch television after nine o'clock? **A.** ....

....

Q. 6 How many videos do you watch every week? **A.** ....

....

True or false? T/F?

1 Angie's favourite programme is 'Pop World'. ☐

2 Angie doesn't often watch 'Sports Day'. ☐

3 She watches television for about two hours every day. ☐

4 She never watches television before she has done her homework. ☐

5 She sometimes watches television after nine o'clock. ☐

6 She never watches videos. ☐

Lesson 15

A Choose and complete

1 One day I might ...write..... a book in English.

A) wrote B) write C) written D) writing

2 When I am eighteen I might .... student.

A) be B) be a C) to be D) will be a

3 Have you typed the article yet? Yes, I ....

A) have typed it already B) have typed C) will type it D) typing it already

4 Do you .... have a lot of homework?

A) then B) every C) every day D) always

5 I watched .... television programme last year.

A) these B) this C) those D) them

6 My .... book is 'The Red Pony'. Do you want to borrow it?

A) good B) better C) favourite D) right

7 .... people in the class have televisions?

A) How much B) How many C) Who D) Whose

8 Have you .... your review yet?

A) did B) written C) write D) do

B Think and decide

I take it to school. I do it every day.
Sometimes I do it at school. I usually do it at home.
What is it? Is it a pet? Is it a sport? Is it homework?

C Write

Put the verb in the past tense.

1 She can walk slowly. She could walk slowly.......................................

2 The monkeys eat lots of bananas. ....

3 She's got a computer at home. ....

4 They choose the best review. ....

5 We come home at five o'clock. ....

6 Our teacher tells us to speak quietly. ....

Lesson 16

A Read and answer

Read the story in your Pupil's Book again.

1 Where did the author find his dog?

....

2 Did he want a pet?

....

3 What did Laika do while he was working in Palomar?

....

4 Why did the author go to Berkeley?

....

5 What happened in the middle of the night?

....

6 What did the author hear outside?

....

7 Did the author rescue his dog?

....

8 Why did he give Laika to his friends?

....

B Choose and complete

cabin	helicopter	earthquake	barking	bang	astronomer	space station

1 I was asleep but I woke up when I heard a loud ......bang.......

2 The dog was .... because a man was knocking at the door.

3 A small house is sometimes called a ....

4 You can fly in a ....

5 Buildings fall down when there is an ....

6 An .... studies the stars.

7 My father works on a .... on the moon.

Read and correct

Correct these sentences so they are true.

1 The man had a cat called Laika. ....The man had a dog called Laika...........

2 The man bought Laika on the road to Palomar. ....

....

3 The man liked animals very much. ....

....

4 He loved Laika but she wasn't a very clever dog. ....

....

5 She always barked while he was working. ....

....

6 One day the man went to Berkeley to do some work so he left Laika at home. ....

....

C Look and write

Look at the pictures and write the first part of the story. Then finish the story.

....

....

....

....

....

....

....

....

Lesson 17

A Discuss and write

1

It might be a pen or a pencil. ....

2

....

....

3

....

....

4

....

....

5

....

....

B Look and write

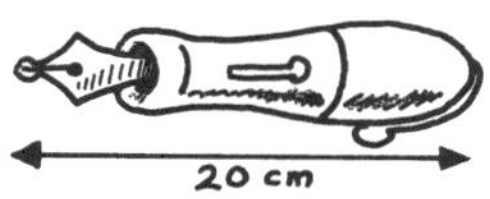

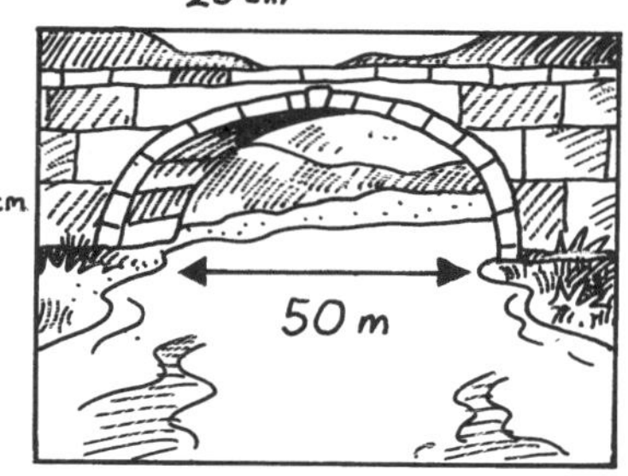

1 The book is twenty centimetres .... long.

2 The river is .... wide.

3 The boy is .... tall.

4 The pen is .... long.

5 The ruler is .... long.

6 The girl is .... tall.

7 The suitcase weighs ....

C Look, match and complete

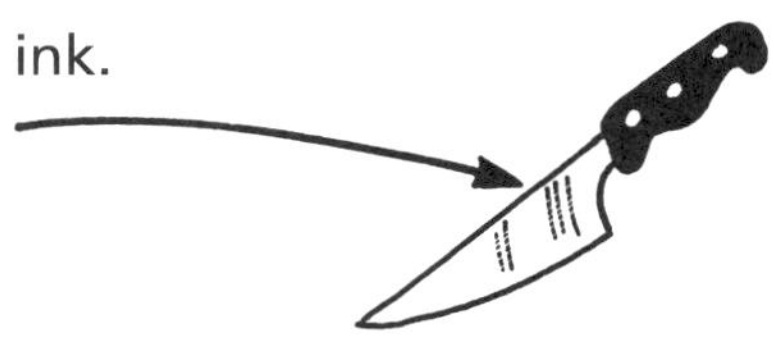

1 It's made of metal. We use it for stirring.
2 People use them a lot in Japan and China. They're for eating with.
3 We use it for taking photographs. It isn't very big, but sometimes it's expensive.
4 You can use it for doing arithmetic very quickly.
5 It's long and thin and we light it with a match.
6 It's for sitting on. It's made of wood, metal or plastic.
7 We use it for writing but it doesn't contain ink.
8 It's made of metal. We use it for cutting.

Now complete the crossword with the names of these things.

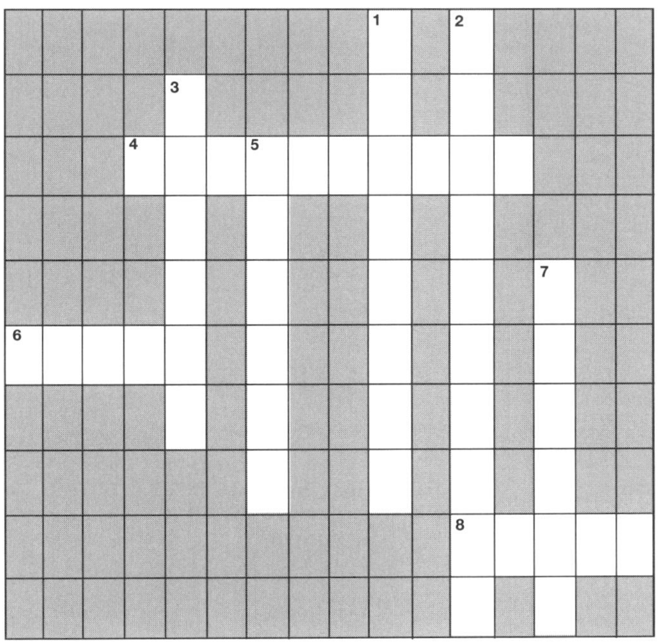

Write and say

Write sentences about these objects. Ask your friend to guess the object.

 1 *It's for eating. It's made of metal.* ....

 2 ....

 3 ....

Lesson 18

A Join

1 She walked into the garden. She was singing. ....She walked into the garden singing.................

2 He came into the room. He was shouting. ....

....

3 My brother was sitting near the window. He was doing his homework. ....

....

4 They were sitting in the restaurant. They were eating hamburgers. ....

....

5 The dog was running up the hill. It was barking. ....

....

6 The children were lying on the floor. They were watching television. ....

....

B Complete

Put the verbs in the past tense.

1 A volcano ....erupted.......................... in Chile in 1994. (erupt)

2 He .... two kilometres every day. (run)

3 The children .... three plates of spaghetti. (eat)

4 The woman .... her calculator in her bag. (find)

5 Last night my sister .... to watch television at nine o'clock. (want)

6 We .... a lot of butter in the cake. (put)

Write

Copy this information about Thailand, adding capital letters and full stops (.).

bangkok is the capital of thailand more than six million people live in bangkok so it is a very crowded city the official language of the country is thai and many people speak chinese

....

....

....

Find out

How many people live in Thailand? ....

Find out three other important things about Thailand.

....

....

....

Find Thailand on a map of the world.

Write three things about your country.

....

....

....

C Choose and write

Find words about food or eating in the box and list them below.

lunch mountain nut egg street breakfast hungry crops meat volcano bread
lava meal oven fork dish postcard ash pyramid potato dinner plate ruler

1 lunch ....

2 ....

3 ....

4 ....

5 ....

6 ....

7 ....

8 ....

9 ....

10 ....

11 ....

12 ....

13 ....

14 ....

15 ....

Which of the words in the box need -es for the plural?

lunch ....

Do you know all the words? If not, look them up in a dictionary.

Lesson 19

A Look and write

Look at this information about the rainfall and temperature in Seoul, Korea.

Answer the questions.

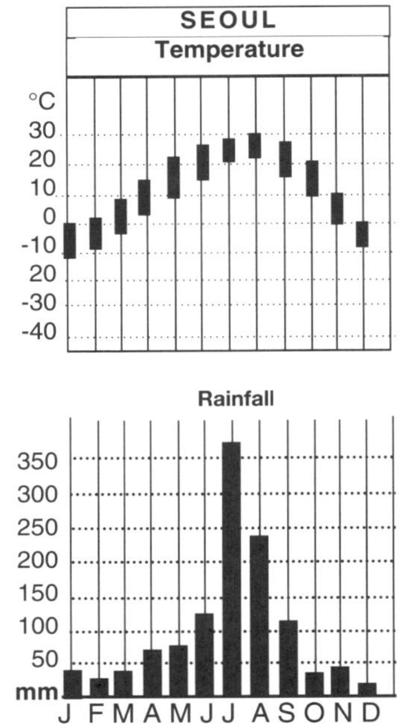

1 Which month has the highest rainfall? July has the highest rainfall.

2 For how many months is the rainfall less than 100 millimetres?

....

3 Which is the driest month? ....

....

4 Which is the hottest month? ....

....

5 Is October wetter than September? ....

6 Is March drier than April? ....

B Read and complete

Read the conversation below and complete Tim's chart.

	Saturday	Sunday	Monday	Tuesday	Wednesday	Thursday	Friday
250 mm							
200 mm							
150 mm				✔			
100 mm							
50 mm							
0 mm							

Tim Hi, Sam. I'm doing a survey of the daily rainfall.

Sam Did it rain yesterday?

Tim Yesterday. Thursday? No, it didn't. But it rained on Monday and on Wednesday. There were two hundred millimetres of rain on Monday and one hundred on Wednesday. Sunday was the wettest day. Two hundred and fifty millimetres of rain.

Sam That's a lot. But it didn't rain at all on Saturday.

Tim No. And today there has only been half a centimetre of rain.

Order and find out

Put the rivers below in alphabetical order. Then put them in page order.

Nile p7	**1** Amazon	**1** Nile ....
Amazon p33	**2**	**2** ....
Yangtze p50	**3**	**3** ....
Mississippi p13	**4**	**4** ....
Danube p29	**5**	**5** ....
Zambezi p43	**6**	**6** ....
Darling p62	**7**	**7** ....
Ganges p22	**8**	**8** ....
Euphrates p54	**9**	**9** ....
Mekong p41	**10**	**10** ....

Which is the longest river in the world? ....

C

Write

Write the figures in words.

1 The Nile is 6,695 km long.

The Nile is six thousand, six hundred and ninety-five kilometres long. ....

2 The Ganges is 2,510 km long.

....

3 The Danube is 2,858 km long.

....

4 The Mississippi is 3,780 km long.

....

5 The Mekong is 4,425 km long.

....

What is the longest river in your country? ....

How long is it? ....

Lesson 20

A

Choose and complete

some the a

Anna and Bill need ...some... information for their school radio programme. They have looked in .... school library but they need more information. There are maps and atlases about .... whole world but they need information about particular countries. Bill wants to do something about Japan. He knows there are .... famous volcanoes in Japan and he wants to find out more. They decide to write .... letter to .... Japanese Information Centre. .... week later they get .... reply from Mr Sato, ... Information Officer.

Choose and complete

Dear Sir, Australia Yours faithfully, Lake Road 12th January 1996 West School Perth

West School

....

....

....

....

We are in Class 3B at West School. We are doing a project about Korea. We would like to have some information about the history and geography of Korea. We are particularly interested in the Korean language. We need the information as soon as possible. We look forward to hearing from you.

....

Sandy and Amy Keen

B

Read and answer

Look at the letter in A.

1. Which class are the children in? The children are in Class 3B.
2. What is the name of their school? ....
3. Which country do they live in? ....

4 What is their project about? ....

5 What are they particularly interested in? ....

....

6 When do they need the information? ....

....

Choose and complete

Information Assistant
your letter
Sandy Amy
Yours sincerely,
Korean Information Centre
Seoul
Korea
information
project

Korean Information Centre
....
....

Dear .... and .... ,

Thank you for .... about Korea.

We are sending you some .... There is also a leaflet about the Korean language.

Good luck with your ....

....

Mrs Han

....

C Read and circle

Two words in each row have similar meanings. Circle them.

1 particularly person address very teacher centre

2 information usually reply quickly facts geography gently

3 answer letter office reply information industry

4 correct quick luck right simple serious

Lesson 21

A Read and answer

Read the story in your Pupil's Book again.

1 Where does Juan live? ....

2 What grows in the hills around the town? ....

....

3 What grows in the valleys? ....

4 How many towns are there around the lake? ....

....

5 Are there many cars and buses in the town? ....

....

6 Why do people usually carry things? ....

....

7 Where is the big house? ....

8 Did Juan's father live in the big house? ....

9 Do you think Juan liked the big house?...

10 What is your favourite place? ....

Decide

True or false? T/F?

1 A ferry boat is a large bus. [F]

2 Corn grows in Guatemala. [ ]

3 San Pablo is in the mountains. [ ]

4 Coffee berries grow in the valleys. [ ]

5 Many people go to work by train. [ ]

6 The big house is near the lake. [ ]

7 A mule is an animal. [ ]

8 Cars are important in San Pablo. [ ]

9 Juan was born in the big house. [ ]

10 Juan's father didn't like his job. [ ]

Write

Write about three differences between your town and San Pablo.

1 ....

2 ....

3 ....

B Read and complete

because so but with if at behind ~~and~~

1 There are high cliffs ....and....... bright fields of corn.
2 San Pablo is on a lake .... seven other towns around it.
3 .... you open the gate you can walk down to the water.
4 People go from one town to another by ferry boat or canoe .... the road isn't good.
5 There aren't many cars .... people have to carry everything.
6 There's a road .... it isn't a good one.
7 .... night Juan likes to go down to the lake.
8 Juan was born in a little house .... the big house.

C Look and write

A

B

1 In A there are a few buses but there aren't any buses in B.
2 In A there are some shops but ....
3 In B there is a river but ....
4 In A there are some bicycles but ....
5 In A there are some cars but ....
6 In B there are lots of trees but ....
7 There are steep hills in B but ....
8 There aren't any people in B but ....

Lesson 22

A Listen and circle

Circle the sentence you hear.

1 The calculator is thirty centimetres long.

The calculator is thirteen centimetres long.

2 In our library there aren't any books about Korea.

In our library there aren't many books about Korea.

3 There are some very famous volcanoes in Japan.

There are some famous volcanoes in Japan.

4 It must be a calculator.

It might be a calculator.

5 She hurried into the street shouting.

She ran into the street shouting.

6 The coldest day was Thursday.

The coldest day was Tuesday.

B Listen and choose

Choose the correct word.

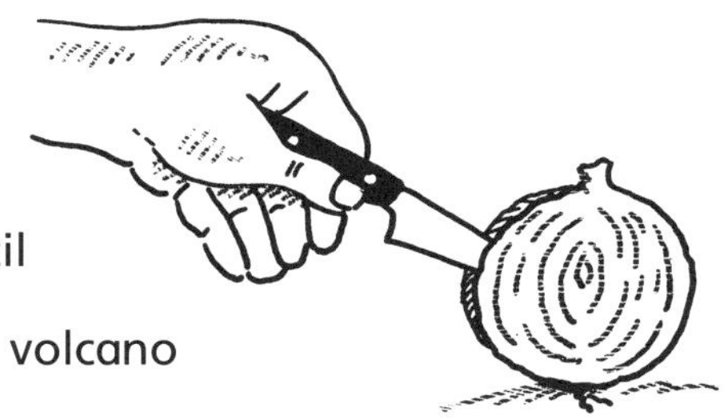

1 A) knife B) ball C) pencil

2 A) café B) calculator C) volcano

3 A) making lunch B) doing a project

C) listening to a radio programme

4 A) pencils B) spoons C) coins

5 A) speak two languages B) have two classes C) watch two programmes

6 A) sunset B) explosion C) hole

C Listen and complete

Listen to the interview and complete the children's questionnaire with Sandy's answers.

QUESTIONNAIRE

Q. Have you ever been to another country?

A. ....

Q. How many countries have you visited?

A. ....

Q. Which country did you like the most?

A. ....

Q. Have you ever been in a plane?

A. ....

Now write down your answers to the questionnaire.
Write down your friend's answers.

YOUR ANSWERS	YOUR FRIEND'S ANSWERS
....	....
....	....
....	....
....	....
....	....
....	....
....	....

Lesson 23

A Choose and complete

1 It ...might... be an old coin but I'm not sure.
A) must B) might C) will D) was

2 We use it for stirring so it .... be a spoon.
A) can B) probably C) must D) would

3 These are called chopsticks. We use them ....
A) for eating B) eating C) to eat D) eating

4 They hurried into the streets .... for their friends.
A) looked B) looking C) looks D) were looking

5 What does screaming ....? It means shouting loudly.
A) means B) meant C) meaning D) mean

6 Let's go .... a walk.
A) for B) to C) with D) in

7 *km* means ....
A) centimetres B) kilometres C) degrees D) pounds

8 Where is this picture from? It .... be from Paris. I can see the Eiffel Tower.
A) must B) is C) could D) might

B Think and decide

You can paint them.
They roll but they don't bounce.
If you want to eat them you break them.
You can cook them in many different ways.
Are they nuts? Are they balls? Are they eggs?

C Write

Complete the sentences with the verb.

1 She was ...walking........... quickly because it was raining. (walk)
2 He was........................ because the story was sad. (cry)
3 The children were .... their sandwiches for lunch. (make)
4 Most people were .... their suitcases with them. (take)
5 We are .... to a new house next month. (move)
6 The teacher came in because the boys were........................ . (shout)
7 I hurt my finger when I was .... a tomato. (cut)

Lesson 24

A Read and answer

Read the story in your Pupil's Book again.

1. How old was Mary? ....
2. Did Mary like the garden? ....
3. What is a robin? ....
4. What do robins eat? ....
5. What did Mary pick up from the ground? ....
6. Where did she put the key? ....
7. What was she doing in the garden the next day? ....
8. What happened when the wind blew? ....
9. What did Mary find under the ivy? ....
10. Did she go into the garden? ....

Read and circle

Circle the odd one out in each row.

1. parrot robin owl eagle snake
2. seed tree plant ivy door tree grass
3. key paper spoon knife coin fork ring
4. wood metal plastic paper wall
5. gardener teacher doctor tin opener taxi driver

B Write

Put the verb in the past tense.

1. The gardener ...pointed... towards a small bird. (point)
2. The robin .... between some flowers, looking for an insect or a worm. (hop)
3. Suddenly Mary .... an object. (see)
4. The robin .... into the tree and Mary .... down to pick up the object. (fly, bend)
5. Mary .... up and .... at the key. (stand, look)
6. She .... the key in her pocket. (put)

C Look, match and write

Match each picture with one of the sentences below.

1 Mary was walking next to the garden. She could see the tops of the trees above the high wall.

2 The robin hopped near Mary. He looked at her.

3 He was looking for an insect or a worm.

4 Suddenly Mary saw an object on the ground. She thought it was a ring.

5 Mary bent down to pick up the object.

6 It was a key. Was it the key to the secret garden?

Finish the story in your own words.

....

....

....

....

....

....

Lesson 25

A Choose and complete

work	~~was~~	knew	am	wanted	worked	was

1 'It is very hot in Thailand.' He said it ....was.... very hot in Thailand.

2 'We want four ice creams.' They said they .... four ice creams.

3 'I know a lot about the environment.' Mary said she .... a lot about the environment.

4 'We .... hard at school.' The children said they .... hard at school.

5 'I .... very hungry.' She said she .... very hungry.

Write

1 'That's a good idea.' What did she say? ....She said it was a good idea.....

2 'I'm very sorry.' What did he say? ....

3 'Jim is very late.' What did she say? ....

4 'She's very interested in maths.' What did he say? ....

....

5 'We are going to the station.' What did they say? ....

....

6 'I like that programme on the radio.' What did she say? ....

....

7 'I feel very tired.' What did the boy say? ....

8 'I can help with the work.' What did the girl say? ....

....

B Think and write

1 **A:** I'm very tired. **B:** ....You should go to bed early.....

2 **A:** I have a maths test tomorrow. **B:** You should ....

3 **A:** I need a book about the rainforest. **B:** ....

4 **A:** I don't like going to school by bus. **B:** ....

5 **A:** I've lost my watch. **B:** ....

6 **A:** I don't understand this word. **B:** ....

7 **A:** I want to buy a new bike. **B:** ....

C Look and write

Look at Gary and Milly's answers to the questionnaire.
Do you agree?

		Gary	Milly
1	Everybody should start school when they are three years old.	✔	
2	Children should have pocket money.	✔	
3	We should be polite to our teachers.	✔	✔
4	We should work hard at school.	✔	✔
5	Everybody should learn a second language.		✔
6	We should do exercise every day.	✔	✔
7	We should study maths every day.		
8	We should cycle to school.		✔

Write down the things Gary agrees with.

1 *Everybody should start school when they are three years old.*

2 ....

3 ....

4 ....

5 ....

Write down the things Milly agrees with.

1 *We should be polite to our teachers.*

2 ....

3 ....

4 ....

5 ....

Write down the things you agree with.

1 ....

2 ....

3 ....

4 ....

5 ....

Lesson 26

A Match

Match the words with similar meanings.

kinds	cut down
hot	woods
rare	warm
destroy	types
forest	unusual

Choose and complete

cut   come   are worried   shouldn't   produce   live   disappear   contain

1 Many different kinds of animal .....live..... in rainforests.
2 If the forests disappear the birds and animals will .... too.
3 Some scientists .... about the rainforests.
4 Farmers .... down rainforests to use the land for cows.
5 Ingredients for some medicines .... from the rainforests.
6 Some people think we .... cut down rainforests.
7 Trees are important because they .... oxygen.
8 Some plants .... ingredients for medicines.

B Write and answer

Add capital letters and full stops (.).

gorillas are the largest kind of ape in the world
they have very wide shoulders, long arms and
short legs they can be 2 metres tall there are three
types of gorilla and they all live in africa
gorillas are friendly animals but they are quite shy
they are in danger of extinction because farmers
are cutting down their forest homes

....

....

....

....

....

1 Where do gorillas live? ....

2 How many types of gorilla are there? ....

3 Are gorillas friendly animals? ....

4 Why are gorillas in danger of extinction? ....

Find out

Which animals are in danger of extinction? Write the names of three here.

1 .... 2 .... 3 ....

Which animals in your country are in danger? Why?

C Read and order

Write ten words from the box below in each list.

Then tick the words you have read in Lesson 26 of the Pupil's Book.

calculator trees plants cow lizard birds flowers radio bananas monkey
horse television parrot video lemons crocodile dog camera corn
onions coffee jaguar orang-utan oranges garlic

Animals		Things that grow	
1 cow	☐	1 trees	☐
2	☐	2	☐
3	☐	3	☐
4	☐	4	☐
5	☐	5	☐
6	☐	6	☐
7	☐	7	☐
8	☐	8	☐
9	☐	9	☐
10	☐	10	☐

Write down the other words from the box. What are these things?

1 ....

2 ....

3 ....

4 ....

5 ....

Lesson 27

A Look and write

1 This animal is a cheetah. It looks like a cat. ....

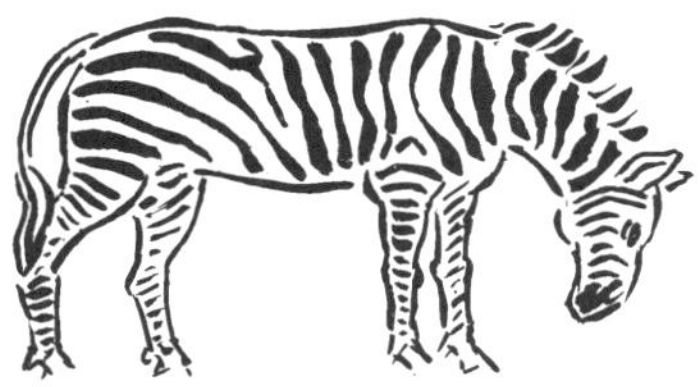

2 This animal is a zebra. ....

3 This animal is a bat. ....

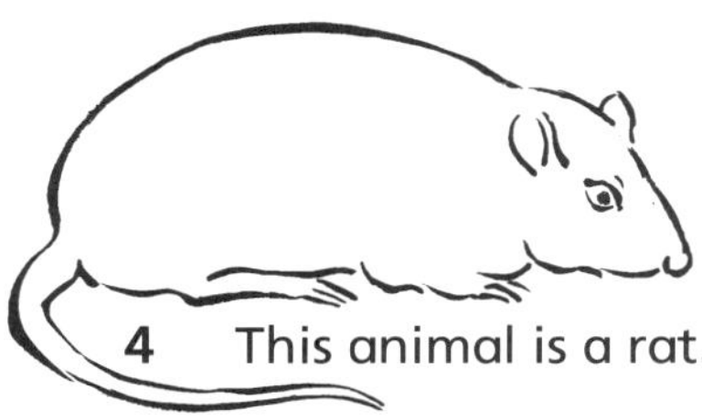

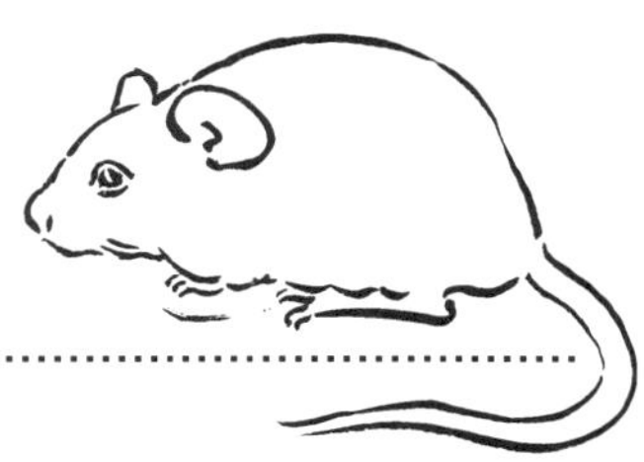

4 This animal is a rat. ....

Look and draw

Draw lines to show where you can find these animals and birds.

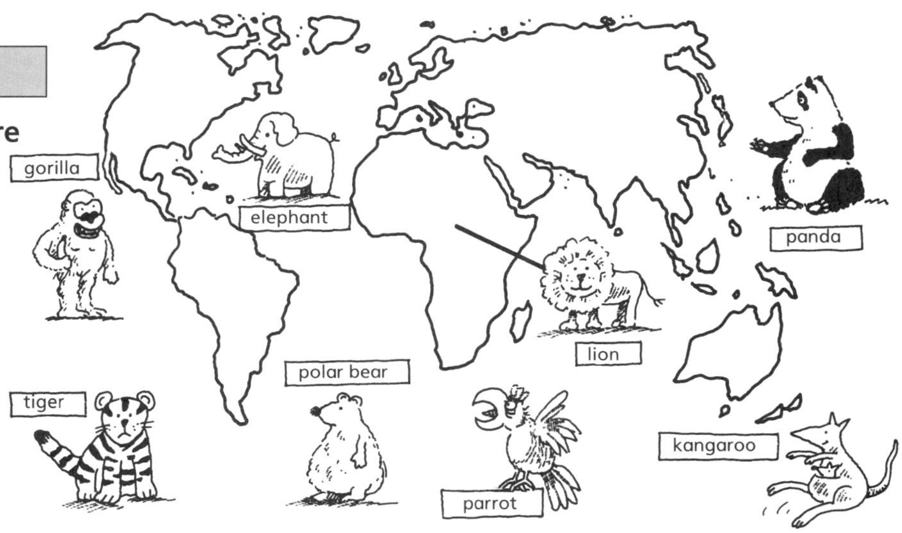

B Read and order

Put these words in alphabetical order:

now	noon	nose	note	none	notice	nut	north	noise	number	not	nurse

1 noise........................ 5 .... 9 ....

2 .... 6 .... 10 ....

3 .... 7 .... 11 ....

4 .... 8 .... 12 ....

Match

Match the meanings with the words.

for example, 1

twelve o'clock

1. to see something
2. a poster or piece of paper telling news or giving information

This person helps people when they are ill.

1. a short letter
2. a sound in music

a part of the body

notice

nose

number

note

nurse

noon

C Complete

Use words from the list at the top of the page to complete these sentences.

1 I heard a loud ...noise............ last night.

2 He has short hair, brown eyes and a small ....

3 I can't remember his address. Is it .... nine, Bridge Street?

4 The teacher will be cross because I did .... do my homework.

5 Our teacher says we have to bring a .... if we are late.

6 The .... on the door says 'The English class is in room 6.'

Lesson 28

A Look and write

Look at Jo's completed questionnaire and write eight sentences.

	Environment questionnaire	always	usually	never
1	Do you recycle paper?		✔	
2	Do you recycle glass?		✔	
3	Do you recycle plastic bottles?			✔
4	Do you recycle cans?		✔	
5	Do you re-use plastic bags?	✔		
6	Do you turn the lights off when you aren't in the room?		✔	
7	Do you save water?		✔	

1 Jo usually recycles paper. ....

2 ....

3 ....

4 ....

5 ....

6 ....

7 ....

B Complete and say

Give it to her. Bring them to us. Give them to him.

Complete these conversations with the sentences above.

a. **Larry** Is this your book?
Sally Yes, it is. But I don't want it. Jane wants it.

....

b. **Alan** Look! I've got three bags of glass bottles. Who's collecting them?
Nick Hiro's collecting them.

....

c. **Sally** Are you collecting old newspapers?
Anna Yes, we are.

....

C Read and answer

Green Circle,
Wood Lane,
Middleplace
6th January

Dear North School Head Teacher,
Are you interested in the environment? Are you interested in recycling? Our name is Green Circle. We organize recycling and we want your help. We are doing a recycling project in your area. We want to put three large bins in your school playground for old paper, cans and glass. You can then collect all these things for recycling. We will empty your bins every week. This will help you and help the environment. If you are interested please write to Jim Wells or Karen White at Green Circle.

Yours sincerely,

Jim Wells

1 What does Green Circle do? *Green Circle organizes recycling.* ....

2 What do they want to do at North School? ....

....

3 When will they empty the bins? ....

4 Who should the head teacher write to? ....

....

5 Do you think this is a good idea? ....

Lesson 29

A Read and answer

Read the story in your Pupil's Book again.

1 Where did the dragon live? ....

2 How do you know the dragon was dangerous? ....

....

3 Who asked the dragon hunter to come and help? ....

....

4 Why were the villagers surprised when they saw the hunter?..

....

5 Did lots of people want to go with the old man? ....

6 What did the men have to do outside the dragon's cave? ....

....

7 How big was the hole? ....

....

8 What did the boy do when the hole was ready? ....

9 What happened to the dragon? ....

....

10 Did the young men kill the dragon? ....

B Write

Put the verb in the past.

1 The old dragon hunter .... a small boy with him. (bring)

2 The men .... a hole for the dragon. (dig)

3 The dragon .... out of the cave. (run)

4 The dragon .... into the hole. (fall)

5 The hunter .... the dragon. (kill)

C Look and write

Look at the leaflet below and write five pieces of advice for looking after rabbits.

Clean your rabbit's cage. | Feed your rabbit regularly. | Hold your rabbit gently. | Cover the cage at night. | Talk quietly to your rabbit.

1 *You should clean your rabbit's cage.* ....

2 ....

3 ....

4 ....

5 ....

Write

1 'Where is the dragon?' the hunter asked the villagers.

The hunter asked the villagers where the dragon was. ....

2 'Where are the rabbits?' the man asked his son.

The man asked his son ....

3 'Where is the waiter?' the woman asked her friend.

She ....

4 'What is the panda's name?' the children asked the zoo-keeper.

The children ....

5 'Where is Mill End Street?' Mary asked the policeman.

Mary ....

6 'What is a periscope?' Jim asked his teacher.

Jim ....

7 'Where are the frying pans?' Dean asked his mother.

Dean ....

8 'What is the homework?' the children asked the teacher.

The children ....

Lesson 30

A Listen and decide

Listen to Angie and Bob's conversation and decide which of the things below they agree or disagree with. Write A (agree) or D (disagree) next to their names.

1 People are always talking about the rainforests.

Angie ☐ Bob ☐

2 Rainforests are important.

Angie ☐ Bob ☐

3 This week's school programme is about an interesting subject.

Angie ☐ Bob ☐

4 Sports programmes are boring.

Angie ☐ Bob ☐

5 The school quizzes are good.

Angie ☐ Bob ☐

Listen and circle

Circle the sentence you hear.

1 Car tyres are made of rubber.

Car tyres are made of wood.

2 We are recycling glass bottles.

We are recycling plastic bottles.

3 Please bring old newspapers to us.

Please give old newspapers to them.

4 If you go to bed early, you won't be tired.

If you go to bed early, you'll be tired.

5 You shouldn't leave your books at home.

You should leave your books at home.

6 Sarah looks like my sister.

Sarah doesn't look like my sister.

B Look, listen and circle

Look at this map. Circle the places you hear and add lines to show where they are.

C Listen and write

These five friends like writing letters. Listen to the cassette and complete the lines to show when they wrote letters last year.

Lesson 31

A Choose and complete

1 ..Nobody.. should waste water.

A) Nobody B) Everybody C) Somebody D) Something

2 Children .... be polite to teachers.

A) shouldn't B) are usually C) should D) often

3 If we cut down rainforests many animals ....

A) are disappearing B) disappeared C) have disappeared D) will disappear

4 Farmers cut down rainforests .... they want to use the land.

A) because B) until C) so D) and

5 Pandas need .... 600 bamboo canes every day.

A) eating B) to eat C) eats D) ate

6 .... ever thrown any litter in the street?

A) You have B) Have you C) You D) Have

7 A zebra .... a horse but it has stripes.

A) looks B) looks like C) likes D) look like

8 .... tigers in this cage?

A) Is there B) Was there C) There any D) Are there any

B Write

1 If we are late we ..won't see.. the film. (see)

2 If you work hard, you .... your exam. (pass)

3 If you speak loudly, I .... you. (hear)

4 If we run fast, we .... the bus. (catch)

5 If they walk up the mountain, they .... very tired. (be)

6 If we write it down, we .... to do it. (forget)

C Write

1 'I'm hungry,' said Kelly. ..Kelly said she was hungry...

2 'I don't like hamburgers,' said Frank. ....

3 'They work very hard,' said Joanna. ....

4 'Mary knows lots of people,' said Anna. ....

....

Lesson 32

A Read and answer

Read the story in your Pupil's Book again.

1 Was Akimbo with John all the time? ....

2 Where was John? ....

3 Did Akimbo know what to do? ....

4 Where was the paddle? ....

5 What did Akimbo do with the paddle? ....

....

6 What did the crocodile do? ....

7 How did John get out of the water? ....

....

8 Was John hurt? ....

9 Why did Akimbo take off his shirt? ....

....

10 Did John stand up and walk? ....

What did Akimbo do next?

....

....

....

....

....

B Read and circle

Circle the words with similar meanings.

1 cry shout mud hole stop

2 afraid happy frightened alone sleepy

3 paddle ear oar boat tree

4 log river bandage piece of wood crocodile

C Look and write

Look at the pictures below and continue the story, using the past tense of these verbs:

swim	get out	run	start	find	go back	rescue

....

....

....

....

....

....

....

....

Lesson 33

A Write

1 My teacher corrects my homework.

My homework is corrected by my teacher.

2 In our group Anna plays the guitar.

In our group the guitar ....

3 In our group Hiro plays the drums.

In our group the drums ....

4 Dean plays the electric guitar.

The electric guitar ....

5 A teacher always helps the children.

The children ....

6 Children play all the instruments.

All the instruments ....

7 Children organize the concerts.

The concerts ....

8 Jack asks the quiz questions.

The quiz questions ....

Say and write

Work with a friend. One person says the sentences below. The other person agrees with them.

1 **A:** I've got a radio. **B:** I've got one, too.

2 **A:** I haven't got a guitar. **B:** I haven't got one, either.

3 **A:** I haven't seen that programme. **B:** ....

4 **A:** I like Japanese music. **B:** ....

5 **A:** I don't like the violin. **B:** ....

6 **A:** I've done a project on computers. **B:** ....

7 **A:** I'm going to learn to play the keyboard. **B:** ....

8 **A:** I don't like loud music. **B:** ....

B Write

1 English is spoken in the United States.

English is spoken in England and Australia, too. .... (England and Australia)

2 Italian is spoken in Italy. .... (Switzerland)

....

3 Spanish is spoken in Spain. .... (Mexico)

4 Arabic is spoken in Egypt. .... (Kuwait)

5 Portuguese is spoken in Portugal. .... (Brazil)

....

6 French is spoken in France. .... (Canada)

....

C Answer and ask

Answer these questions and then ask your friend.

1 How many days are there in a week?

There are seven days in a week. ....

2 How many seasons are there in a year?

....

3 How many months are there in a year?

....

4 How many days are there in September?

....

5 How many months are there between May and October? ....

....

6 How many hours are there in a day?

....

7 How many minutes are there in an hour?

....

Lesson 34

A Join

Join these sentences using *which*.

1 A piano is a traditional instrument. It doesn't use electricity.
A piano is a traditional instrument which doesn't use electricity.

2 A keyboard is a modern instrument. It looks like a piano.
....

3 The recorder is a simple instrument. It is easy to learn.
....

4 The elephant is a very large animal. It lives in hot countries.
....

5 A parrot is a bird. It has bright feathers.
....

6 A whale is a large animal. It lives in the sea.
....

7 A tiger is a dangerous animal. It eats meat.
....

8 Chopsticks are long thin sticks. They are used for eating.
....

9 The panda is a large bear. It lives in China.
....

10 The charango is a string instrument. It is played in South America.
....

Write

1 She writes this music for children. This music is written for children.
2 He makes the instrument out of pieces of wood. The instrument ....
....
3 He glues the pieces together. The pieces ....
4 He cuts the wood. The wood ....
5 We call this part the neck. This part ....
6 He cuts the soundhole in the front. The soundhole ....
7 He glues the back on. The back ....
8 He fits the head last. The head ....

B Write

Write these sentences, adding capital letters and full stops (.) or question marks (?).

1 spanish guitars are famous

....

2 the violin is a string instrument which is played with a bow

....

3 is your recorder from japan

....

4 mrs williams teaches the recorder at our school

....

5 good instruments are usually expensive

....

C Look and write

What are these things made of?

	wood	paper	plastic	nylon
guitars	✓			
guitar strings				✓
books		✓		
pencils	✓			
pens			✓	
tables	✓			

1 *Guitars are made of wood.* ....

2 ....

3 ....

4 ....

5 ....

6 ....

Lesson 35

A Choose and complete

watch squirrel match giraffe mouse keyboard chopsticks ruler

1 An animal which has a long neck is called a giraffe.
2 An electronic instrument which looks like a piano is called a ....
3 A clock which you wear around your wrist is called a ....
4 The things which are used for eating in China are called ....
5 The thing which is used to control a computer is called a ....
6 A small animal which has a bushy tail is called a ....
7 A wooden stick which is used for measuring is called a ....
8 A very small wooden stick which is used to light candles is called a ....

B Complete and say

too yet now ago

Ellie Hello, Jim. How are you?
Jim Fine, thanks. Do you like your new teacher?
Ellie Yes, he's very nice. But his lessons are too difficult.
Jim But you started a year .... What are you playing ....?
Ellie I can't remember what it's called. It's a song by The Movers.
Jim Great. Can I come and listen to you? I like The Movers.
Ellie No, you can't! I haven't done any practice ....

C Read and order

Put each word in the correct list. (Some words will go in two lists.)

big awful sun tree huge sing fish shout speak hungry think
thin guitar old new cold hot buy fly recorder ice cream
table ancient jeans shoes sleep eat paper clip go green cat
whale angry brown blue sit leave foreign

Verbs (actions)	Nouns (things)	Adjectives (describing words)
....	....	....
....	....	....
....	....	....
....	....	....
....	....	....
....	....	....
....	....	....
....	....	....
....	....	....
....	....	....
....	....	....
....	....	....
....	....	....
....	....	....
....	....	....

How many words are there in each list?

....

How many words are in two lists?

....

Lesson 36

A Read and answer

Read this letter and answer the questions.

North School
15th April

Dear Mr Green,
We received Mr Knight's letter of 10th April. We understand that you cannot give us free tickets for The Movers concert. We are very pleased that the winner of our quiz will be able to visit the Radio Room during the concert. Please could you tell us what time the winner should arrive and who to ask for. We look forward to hearing from you.
Yours sincerely,
Bill and Lisa

1 Who is the letter to?

....

2 When did Mr Knight write to Bill and Lisa?

....

3 Can Mr Green give them free tickets for the concert?

....

4 What do Bill and Lisa want to know?

....

B Match

free	quiz	winner	prize	ticket

1 Something which you need to buy if you are going to a concert. ....ticket....

2 A small competition. ....

3 You don't have to pay for something if it is ... .

4 The person who does the best in a competition. ....

5 Something which is given to the winner. ....

C Say and complete

Laura Shall we go to The Movers concert? I think it'll be great.

Leo I can't go at 7.30. I go to a music class on Saturday evenings.

Laura Yes, but there is a concert at two thirty as well.

Leo Two thirty! Great! How much are the tickets?

Laura The cheapest are £5.

Leo But you can't see anything from the cheapest seats.

Laura The next ones are £10.

Leo That isn't too expensive. Shall we get those?

Laura Fine. But I can't go on the 14th or the 21st.
I'll be on holiday then.

Leo What about the 28th?

Laura That's fine. Yes.

Leo OK. Let's fill in the form.

The Movers

Only six concerts:

Saturday 14th, 21st and 28th June

at 2.30 pm and 7.30 pm

Tickets at £5, £10 or £15.

Please complete the form for tickets.

Complete Laura's form for tickets.

Surname ....Owen....

First name ....Laura....

Address ....7, Willow Street, Northtown....

Number of tickets ....

Date of concert ....

Time ....

Price of ticket .... Total price ....

Look and answer

1 How many tickets does Julie want?

....

2 Is she going to the evening concert?

....

3 When is she going?

....

4 Does she want the cheapest tickets?

....

Surname ....Stone....

First name ....Julie....

Address ....6, Yellow Street, Northtown....

Number of tickets ....3....

Date of concert ....14th June....

Time ....7.30 pm....

Price of ticket ....£15.... Total price ....£45....

Lesson 37

A Read and answer

Read the story in your Pupil's Book again.

1 Did Beth like playing the piano?

....

2 What did Mr Laurence invite the girls to do?

....

3 Was the piano in Mr Laurence's study?

....

4 Was Beth shy?

....

5 Did Beth want Mr Laurence to listen to her playing the piano?

....

6 Why was Beth excited?

....

7 Did Beth go to Mr Laurence's house often?

....

8 How did Beth thank Mr Laurence?

....

9 Did Beth take her present to Mr Laurence's study?

....

B Write

1 She felt very happy. She sang happily.
2 The teacher was angry. She shouted ....
3 The children were very noisy. They did their work ....
4 You are very careful. You have made this very ....
5 The old man was very kind. He looked at her ....
6 The child was shy. She spoke very .... to her teacher.
7 The music was very quiet. He played his guitar ....
8 The journey by train was quick. They arrived very ....

Read and write

Read about these friends. Then write each name in the correct circle below.

Pete and Jim like playing the guitar.
Jim and Wally both play the piano, but Wally can't play the guitar. Sami sometimes plays the piano with Jim but he also likes playing the guitar with Pete.
Marta sometimes plays the piano while Sami's brother, Ahmed, plays the guitar.
She can play the guitar too, but Ahmed can't play the piano.

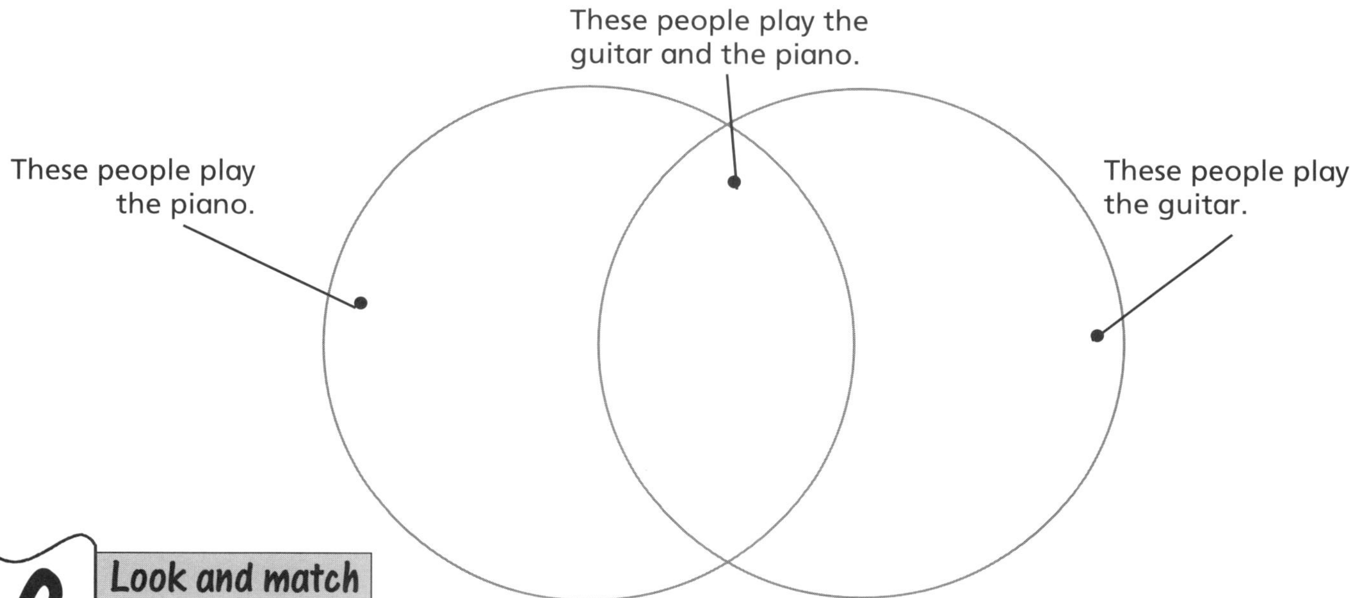

C Look and match

1 When Juanita was six years old her aunt gave her a recorder.

2 Juanita played it every day.

3 One day her uncle took her to a concert. There were instruments from many different countries.

4 At the end of the concert somebody played the drums. Juanita loved them.

5 After that she didn't want to play her recorder. She wanted to play the drums!

Lesson 38

A Listen and circle

Circle the sentence you hear.

1 Who won the music quiz?

Who will win the music quiz?

2 This instrument is played in South America.

This instrument comes from South America.

3 Tammy hasn't done her homework, either.

Tom hasn't done his homework, either.

4 Pencils are made of wood.

A pencil is made of wood.

5 This is a book which I really like.

This is a song which I really like.

B Listen and choose

Choose the correct word.

1 A) knife B) violin C) drum D) flute

2 A) kitchen B) study C) playground D) bedroom

3 A) socks B) scarves C) handkerchiefs D) gloves

4 A) crash B) note C) envelope D) vowel

5 A) telephone book B) address book C) diary D) dictionary

6 A) leg B) neck C) string D) head

7 A) mouse B) cat C) screen D) fish

8 A) instrument B) clock C) desk D) log

9 A) camera B) frying pan C) electric guitar D) calculator

10 A) saxophone B) keyboard C) screen D) violin

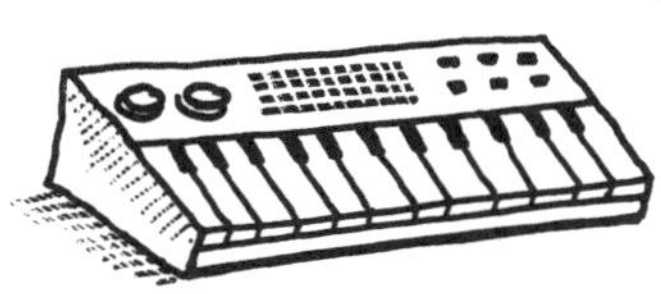

C Listen, draw and write

Listen to the cassette and draw what you hear.

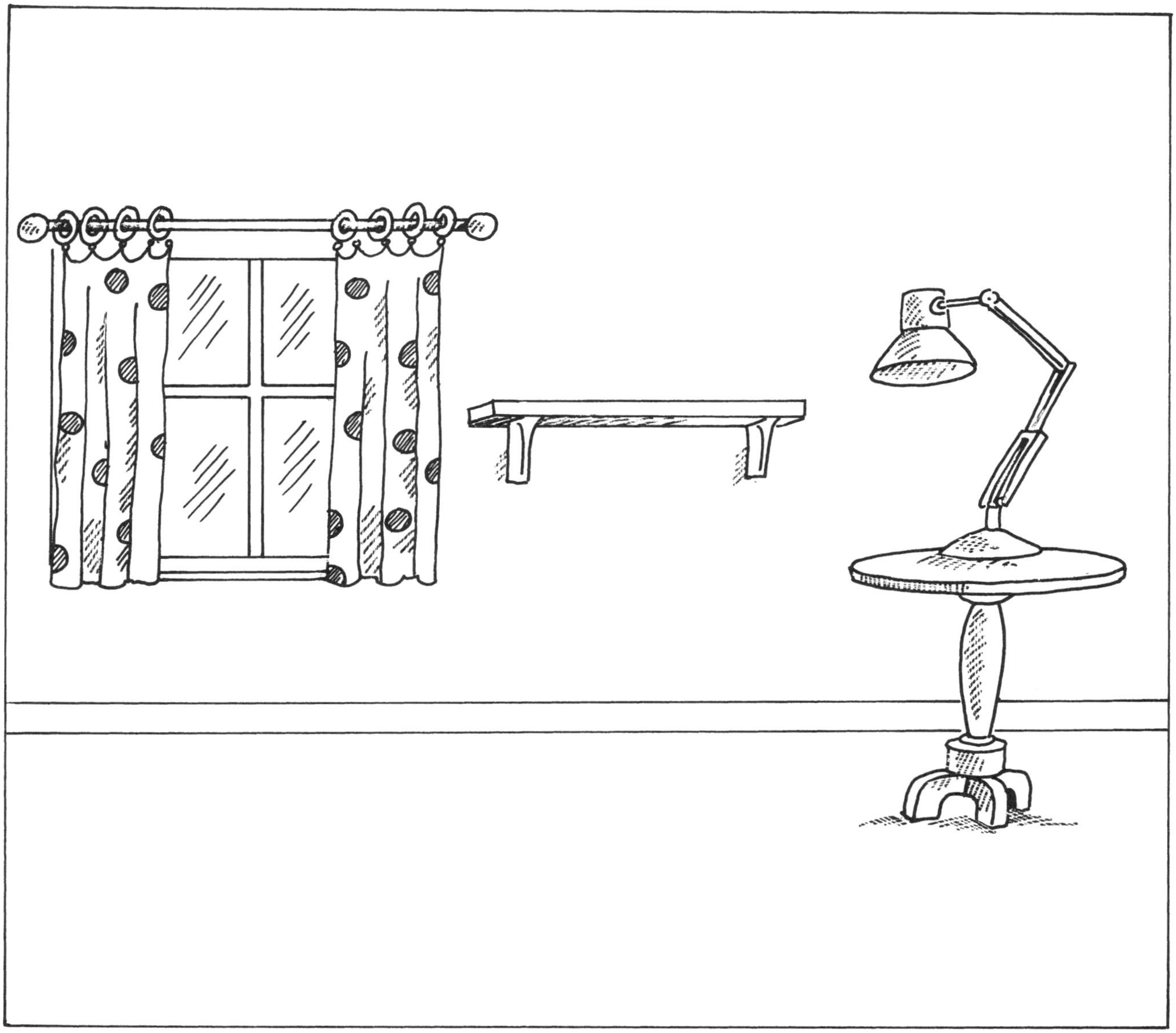

Now write about the picture.

1 The small plant is ....on................................ the table.

2 The black cat is .... the basket.

3 The chair ....

4 The books ....

5 The sofa ....

Lesson 39

A Choose and complete

1 French ....is spoken...... in France.

A) speak B) is spoken C) speaks D) spoken

2 The concerts .... by the children.

A) is organized B) are organized C) organized D) organizes

3 She's got a guitar. I've got one, ...

A) either B) too C) two D) together

4 The recorder is an instrument .... is easy to play.

A) it B) who C) which D) what

5 This part of the guitar .... the neck.

A) called B) is called C) calls D) is calling

6 This model is made .... plastic.

A) of B) on C) out D) under

B Complete and say

countries guitar concert too note already

Anna Hello, Sam. Where are you going?

Sam Hi, Anna. I'm going to a ...concert.......

Anna Who's playing?

Sam I am! I'm playing the guitar.

Anna Oh, I like the .... Do you sing, ...?

Sam Oh no. I can't sing a .... My friend Lizzie sings.

Anna I like singing.

Sam Why don't you come? We're going to play songs from different ....

Anna That's a nice idea.

Sam We're going to play 'Music Speaks Louder Than Words'.

Anna Great! I know that one ....

C Discuss

Do you know any songs from different countries?

Can you sing 'Music Speaks Louder Than Words'?

What is your favourite song?

Lesson 40

A Read and answer

Read the story in your Pupil's Book again.

1 What did Mrs Lawson put in the children's basket?

....

2 What did the children want to find near the railway tracks?

....

3 Who first noticed something very strange?

....

4 Who wanted to go home?

....

5 What crashed down and blocked the railway tracks?

....

6 What did the children use to make flags?

....

7 Who wanted to have two flags? Why?

....

8 Why did Peter shout at Bobbie when the train was coming?

....

9 Did the train stop?

....

B Read and complete

stop	~~saw~~	waved	crash	knew	make	blocked	used

Brave children rescue train!

Last Wednesday three children cleverly prevented a terrible accident. They were going on a picnic when they ....*saw*........ trees and earth crashing onto the railway tracks. The tracks were .... They .... that the next train would .... if they didn't .... it. They .... their scarves and sticks to .... red flags. Then they stood very near the tracks and .... the flags at the driver. Fortunately the driver saw them in time and he was able to stop the train.

C Write

Bobbie wrote about the children's adventure. Finish her story.

Last Wednesday I went on a picnic with my brother and sister. My mother...

....

....

....

....

....

....

....

....

....

....

Read and circle

Circle the odd one out in each row.

1 lunch dinner sandwich breakfast

2 basket tree cherry flower apple grass

3 move crash fall earth wave run

4 brother sister mother father driver daughter

5 bridge tunnel station tracks scarf engine

Complete

too either

1 Mrs Lawson put the sandwiches in the basket. She put the scarves in the basket, *too*..................

2 Peter was waving a flag. Bobbie was waving a flag, ...

3 Bobbie didn't have a watch. Phyllis didn't have a watch, ...

4 Peter heard a noise. Bobbie heard a noise, ...

5 Phyllis was shouting. Bobbie was shouting, ...

6 The driver didn't hear Peter. He didn't hear Phyllis, ...

Lesson 41

A Write

Write the negative sentence.

1 She looks after herself. She *doesn't look after herself.* ....

2 I look after myself. I ....

3 He looks after himself. He ....

4 We look after ourselves. We ....

5 They look after themselves. They ....

6 You look after yourself. You ....

Look and write

What sports can you see here?

1 *swimming*

2 ....

3 ....

4 ....

5 ....

6 ....

7 ....

8 ....

B Decide and write

Decide which of these sentences needs the word *to*.

1 Let's .... do our homework before we watch television.

2 I want .... make a chocolate cake.

3 Shall we .... organize a swimming party?

4 We want .... write a letter to the Safety Information Officer.

5 We are going .... make a radio programme for our school.

6 Shall we .... walk to school or catch the bus?

7 Let's .... go to the library at five o'clock.

8 They want .... do a project about endangered animals.

9 Can I .... have some money for lunch, please?

10 He wants .... write an article about our school radio.

C Look and answer

Maria Bryant

Q. Do you do exercise more than once a week? No, I don't.

Q. Do you walk or cycle to school? No, I catch the bus.

Q. Are you careful when you ride your bike? Yes, I am.

Q. Do you eat lots of fresh fruit? I sometimes eat apples.

Q. Do you eat vegetables and salads? I eat salad once a week.

Q. Do you eat fish as well as meat? No, I don't eat fish or meat. I'm a vegetarian.

Q. How many cans of fizzy drink do you drink each week? About ten.

Q. How many packets of crisps do you eat each week? Five or six.

1 Do you think Maria looks after herself? ....

2 How does she go to school? ....

3 Does she do a lot of exercise? ....

4 Does she eat meat? ....

5 Do you think she eats too many crisps? ....

6 Do you think she drinks too many cans of fizzy drink? ....

Give Maria four pieces of advice.

1 You should do more exercise.

2 You should ....

3 ....

4 ....

Lesson 42

A Join

1 Never run into the road. It is dangerous.

It is dangerous to run into the road.

2 Don't sit on the back of a bicycle. It is dangerous.

It is dangerous ....

3 Never cycle with your hands behind your back. It is silly.

....

4 Have a bell on your bicycle. It is useful.

....

5 Wear bright clothes if you cycle at night. It is safer.

....

6 Always cross the road at zebra crossings. It is better.

....

B Read and decide

Read this information about training your dog.

Some dogs live in the home as members of the family. Others live outside and are guard dogs. But you should always train a dog carefully. This means you must teach it some simple instructions. When you take your dog for a walk, always use a lead so it can't run away. When the dog is very young you will have to be very patient. Before you cross a road, you must tell your dog to sit. Say 'Stop!' or 'Sit!' loudly. Wait until the dog sits. Don't hurry. When the dog sits, look right and left carefully. When there are no cars, cross the road. If the dog does this well, say 'Good dog' so it knows it has done the right thing.

True or false? T/F?

1 Dogs always live outside. F
2 It is important to train young dogs.
3 It is sensible to use a lead when you take a dog for a walk.
4 It is important to be impatient with a young dog.
5 You should tell your dog to sit after you cross a road.

C Look and write

Write eight instructions for this simple potato and parsley recipe.

1 ....

2 ....

3 ....

4 ....

5 ....

6 ....

7 ....

8 ....

CHILDREN'S LIBRARY

Opening hours

Monday	10 am - 1 pm *
Tuesday	10 am - 4 pm **
Wednesday	10 am - 4 pm
Thursday	10 am - 4 pm **
Friday	10 am - 7 pm

* *Storytelling for under-fives 11 am*

** *School groups only 1 pm - 3 pm*

Look and answer

1 Which day does the library close at lunchtime? The library closes at lunchtime on Monday.

2 Which afternoons are for school groups only?

....

3 Which day does the library stay open late?

....

4 What time does the library open in the mornings?

....

5 Which day is storytelling? ....

Lesson 43

A Look, say and write

Tell your friend how to go from Park Road School to the Sports Centre. Then your friend can tell you how to go from Park Road School to the post office.

Write down instructions from Park Road School to the library.

....

....

....

....

....

....

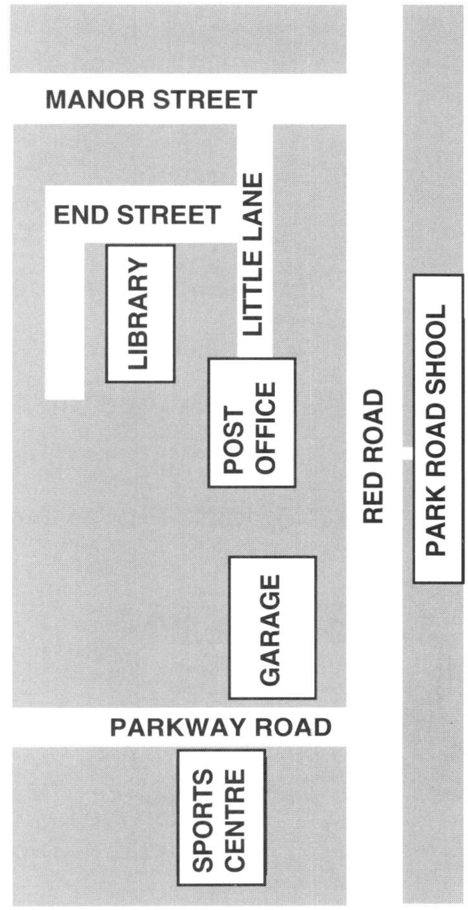

Complete and say

That's fine	I'm sorry	it was	might be	I can't

Louise Hello. Can I join the Computer club, please?

Librarian How old are you?

Louise I'm ten.

Librarian Oh yes. ....That's fine.............

Louise Can I come on Thursday, then?

Librarian Oh no. .... We don't have Computer club on Thursdays. It's on Fridays.

Louise Oh dear. My friend said .... on Thursdays.

Librarian I'm sorry. It isn't. The library is open on Thursdays but the Computer club is on Fridays. Why don't you come on Friday?

Louise .... I play football on Fridays.

Librarian I'm sorry. It .... on Thursdays next year.

B Read and choose

Geography History Science People Sport

Decide which section of the library you should go to for these books:

1. Canada - Climate and Countryside ......Geography......
2. A Simple Guide to Chemistry ....
3. World Deserts ....
4. A Day in the Life of a Policeman ....
5. Famous Pop Stars ....
6. How We Lived One Thousand Years Ago ....
7. Get it Right! Better Swimming for all Ages ....
8. Football: How to Improve ....

C Read and order

Put these sports in alphabetical order, and circle the ones you play. Look up the ones you don't know in a dictionary.

handball badminton swimming gymnastics volleyball tennis
athletics rugby table tennis squash cycling ice skating skiing
football baseball basketball hockey

1. badminton..........................
2. ....
3. ....
4. ....
5. ....
6. ....
7. ....
8. ....
9. ....
10. ....
11. ....
12. ....
13. ....
14. ....
15. ....
16. ....
17. ....

Lesson 44

A Choose and complete

myself (crossed out) yourself himself herself ourselves themselves

1 I am going to type this letter myself.
2 They made the radio programmes ....
3 He has written the report ....
4 We organized most of the things ....
5 She couldn't type very well but she did all the articles ....
6 You have done most of the work ....

B Write

1 What have you done today? (write/book review)
I have written a book review.
2 What has he done today? (write/letter)
....
3 What have they done today? (write/report)
....
4 What has she done today? (finish/story)
....
5 What have Lisa and Hiro done today? (do/interview)
....
6 What has Jill done today? (type/report)
....
7 What have Bill and Jane done today? (make/radio programme)
....
8 What have you done today? (do/an exercise)
....

Look and discuss

Tick the things on this list that you have done today.

- brushed your teeth ☐
- cleaned your shoes ☐
- eaten an apple ☐
- spoken in class ☐
- learnt a new word in English ☐
- done your homework ☐
- ridden your bicycle ☐
- sung a song ☐
- played football ☐
- written a letter ☐
- washed your hair ☐
- had supper ☐
- watched television ☐

Now ask your friend questions. Talk about your lists.

C Look and write

Look at these pictures of Mark and Sarah's trip to the museum. Then write a short report about the trip.

....

....

....

....

....

....

Lesson 45

A Read and answer

Read the story in your Pupil's Book again.

1 Where was Christopher standing with his father? ....

....

2 How many people were there at the football match? ....

....

3 What were the other people doing? ....

4 What was the English team's problem? ....

....

5 Where were Christopher's football boots? ....

6 What colour was his football shirt? ....

7 Did Christopher go onto the field? ....

8 Did he save his first goal? ....

9 What did the captain tell Christopher to do? ....

....

10 How do you know this story was all a dream? ....

....

B Write

Put the verb in the past continuous.

1 All the people ....*were shouting.*.... (shout)

2 Christopher .... at the football match with his father. (stand)

3 The Brazilians .... towards the goal. (run)

4 The ball .... towards the goal. (come)

5 He .... through the air. (dive)

6 He .... his pyjamas. (wear)

C Look and order

Number these pictures in the correct order so they show the story from the Pupil's Book.

Match

1 football

2 cycling

3 golf

4 swimming

5 tennis

6 hockey

Lesson 46

A Listen, look and decide

Listen to Nina and decide where her directions are for.

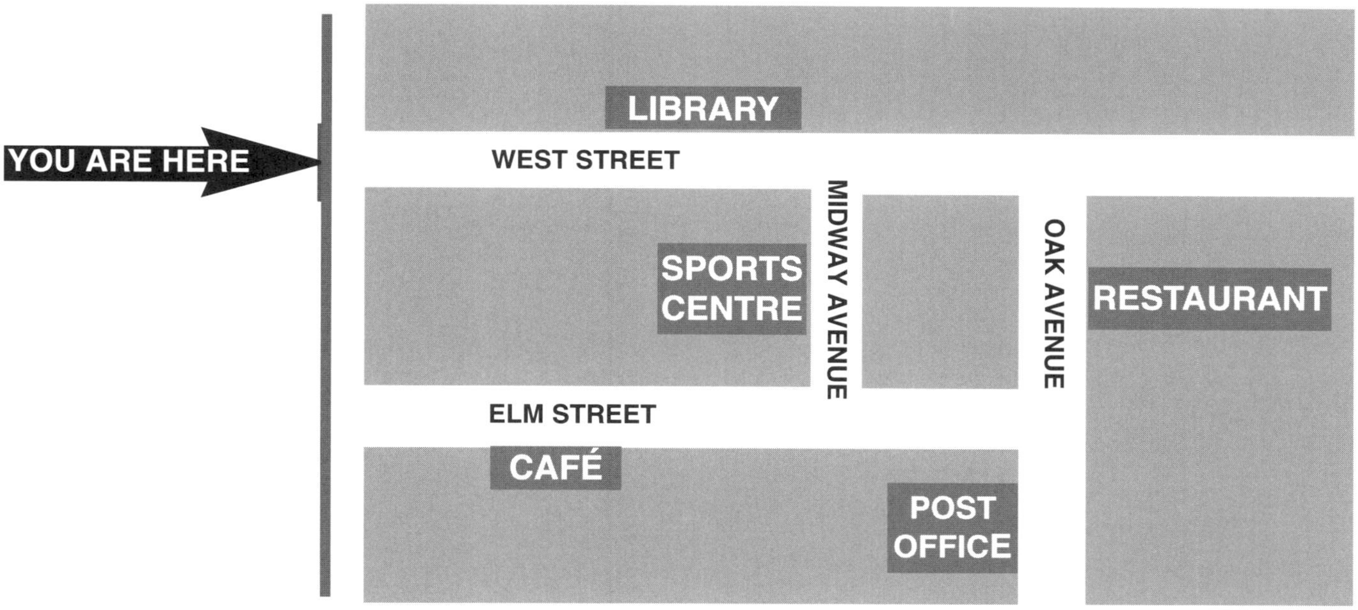

B Listen and complete

Listen to the clues and complete the crossword.

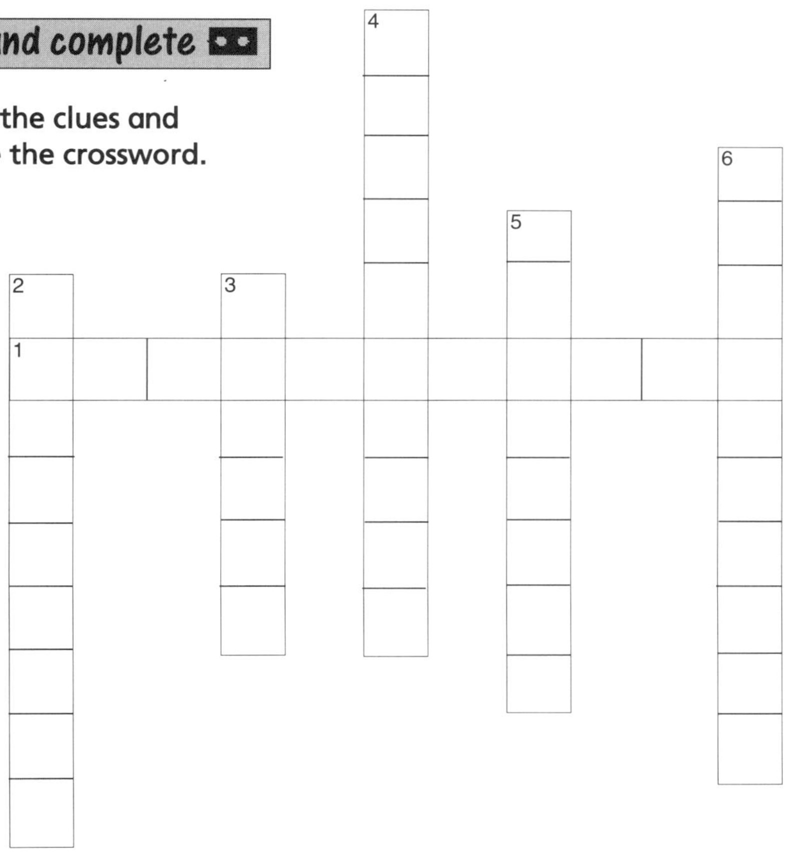

C Listen and complete

people articles music talks library prize teachers project school

This year we decided to make radio programmes for our ......school...... Six of us worked together because there was a lot to do. It was a very useful .... but we had to work very hard. We wrote .... and organized .... for the programmes. We went to the .... and we wrote to different .... Our .... were very pleased with us. We all enjoyed it very much. I think the school liked the .... quiz the best because the .... was great!

Listen and circle

Circle the sentence you hear.

1 Turn right down Silver Street.

Turn left down Silver Street.

2 It is silly to carry a passenger on your bike.

It is sensible to carry a passenger on your bike.

3 I did this myself.

He did this himself.

4 Always turn the lights off when you leave a room.

Never turn the lights off when you leave a room.

5 You don't look after yourself.

You don't look after yourselves.

Lesson 47

A Choose and complete

1 She doesn't look after ...herself.........

A) herself B) himself C) myself D) yourself

2 I don't like pears but I .... apples.

A) eat sometimes B) sometimes C) sometimes eat D) sometimes eats

3 Do you think I eat .... crisps?

A) too many B) too much C) a lot D) too

4 .... eat lots of fruit and vegetables.

A) Shouldn't you B) You should never C) You should D) Should you

5 .... you take your dog for a walk always use a lead.

A) So B) When C) Because D) Until

6 It .... bright clothes at night when cycling.

A) is safer to wear B) safer to wear C) safer D) is safe

7 .... do that! It's dangerous.

A) Do B) Don't C) Always D) Don't do

8 Computer club is .... Thursdays.

A) on B) in C) at D) for

B Look and act out

C Think and say

Tell someone how to get to your house from your school.

Lesson 48

A Read and answer

Read the story in your Pupil's Book again.

1 Why did people call the man in the story 'Mighty One'? ....

....

2 Why did he want to go to Tokyo?..

....

3 What did he see when he was in the forest? ....

4 Where did Kuniko carry Mighty One? ....

....

5 What did Kuniko's grandmother do when she hit her toe on a tree? ....

....

6 How did Mighty One get ready for the competition? ....

....

7 Did Mighty One win the competition? ....

8 Did Mighty One want to win more wrestling competitions? ....

Read and decide

True or false? T/F?

1 This is a true story. [F]
2 Wrestling is a Japanese sport. [ ]
3 Kuniko is the name of the youngest woman in the story. [ ]
4 Old people are stronger than young people. [ ]
5 It is easy to carry a cow. [ ]
6 Mighty One liked Kuniko and her grandmother. [ ]
7 The winners of competitions are often given prizes. [ ]
8 Thunder makes a loud noise. [ ]

B Complete

tired strong weak ~~brave~~ open asleep happy cold best

1 Mighty One was a ...*brave*........ man and a .... fighter.
2 Kuniko said he looked .... so she wanted to carry him.
3 Grandmother was .... in a little house. The door was ....
4 Kuniko said they must cook some rice for a .... man.
5 Mighty One swam in the .... river and got stronger.
6 He won the competition for the .... wrestler.
7 When he won the competition, Mighty One felt very ....

Write

1 'My name's Mighty One.'

He said .... his name was Mighty One. ....

2 'My Grandmother is asleep.'

The girl said her ....

3 'He isn't strong at all.'

Grandmother said ....

4 'You are ready for the Emperor's wrestling competition.'

They said ....

C Look and write

Look at the pictures and tell the first part of the story.

....

....

Finish telling the story.

....

Lesson 49

Work with a partner.
Say a number. Ask a question or give a clue from page 92. Choose the correct answer on page 93.

1 Where can you borrow books? 	2 Which language is spoken in Japan?	3 How many letters are there in the alphabet?	4 Which month is after May?	5 What does a plant need? 
6 This is a machine which can print words.	7 A machine for talking to people.	8 A place which is hot and rainy with lots of trees.	9 A funny film.	10 A drink made from beans which grow in hot countries.
11 A small plastic thing which is used to control a computer.	12 A small thing which is made of metal.	13 A mountain which erupts.	14 Which month is before November?	15 You can see these in the sky at night.
16 A parrot is one. 	17 It is for lighting candles.	18 What is the most important city in a country?	19 A game in which you kick a ball.	20 A very large animal which lives in the sea.
21 If you are ill you sometimes need this.	22 It looks like a horse but it has stripes. 	23 You can recycle this.	24 It's a musical instrument which is often played by pop singers.	25 It means the one I like the best.
26 You pay for this for a concert.	27 It is made of meat. People eat it with chips.	28 It is the opposite of safe.	29 At night you must use them on your bicycle.	30 If you get more than the other team you will win.

1	A) a library	B) a zoo	C) a supermarket
2	A) Chinese	B) Japanese	C) French
3	A) 26	B) 36	C) 16
4	A) July	B) June	C) January
5	A) milk	B) water	C) tea
6	A) a washing machine	B) a car	C) a computer
7	A) a match	B) a telephone	C) a clock
8	A) a city	B) a rainforest	C) a country
9	A) a cartoon	B) an animal	C) music
10	A) coffee	B) lemonade	C) milk
11	A) a colt	B) a mouse	C) a monkey
12	A) money	B) a coin	C) expensive
13	A) a pen	B) a volcano	C) an oven
14	A) December	B) October	C) September
15	A) stars	B) sun	C) plants
16	A) a bird	B) a plant	C) a flower
17	A) a stick	B) a jug	C) a match
18	A) capital	B) village	C) town
19	A) football	B) volleyball	C) tennis
20	A) a penguin	B) a whale	C) an elephant
21	A) medicine	B) problem	C) rubber
22	A) a cat	B) a zebra	C) an alligator
23	A) coffee	B) milk	C) paper
24	A) a guitar	B) a recorder	C) a computer
25	A) interesting	B) popular	C) favourite
26	A) an address	B) a ticket	C) a form
27	A) a cake	B) a hamburger	C) chocolate
28	A) accident	B) dangerous	C) pedestrian
29	A) helmets	B) lights	C) wheels
30	A) tickets	B) kicks	C) points

Lesson 50

A Look and answer

Clothes for kids

T-shirts Code 6758 (all T-shirts fit boys and girls)
Colours: green, red, blue, white, pink

Prices	
Age 2 – 4	£4.50
5 – 7	£6.50 (not in white)
8 – 9	£7.00
10 – 12	£7.50 (not in pink)

With your name printed on the T-shirt -£1.50 extra

1 How much is a T-shirt for a 6-year-old? ....

2 How much is a T-shirt for a 9-year-old if you have the name printed on it? ....

3 Can you get a pink T-shirt for an 11-year-old? ....

4 Can you get a yellow T-shirt for a 3-year-old? ....

5 What colours can you get for 5-7-year-olds? ....

B Read and complete

Read the conversation below and complete the order form for Bill.

Name: Bill Mason

Address: 5, Willow Way, Northtown

Telephone: 588 6235

Item	Code	Colour	Age	Price
....	....	....	....	....

Anna Look, Bill. Do you like these T-shirts?

Bill They're great.

Anna Which colour do you like the best?

Bill Red. It's a good colour for a T-shirt. Or green.

Anna I like the green ones.

Bill Yes, OK. I'll have a green one. I'll need the biggest one because I'm twelve years old.

C Choose and complete

1 They said they ....liked.......... the painting.

A) doesn't like B) liked C) likes D) wasn't

2 If it rains today I .... for a walk.

A) won't go B) go C) goes D) don't go

3 In the school band the piano is .... by Luke.

A) play B) plays C) played D) playing

4 This is a letter .... I wrote last year.

A) which B) who C) when D) what

5 Mary hasn't done her homework, and Jane hasn't done hers ....

A) too B) or C) either D) already

6 The house isn't on the right so it .... on the left.

A) might be B) might C) must D) must be

Join

Join each word with its opposite.

huge	late
quiet	safe
easy	difficult
sensible	tiny
dangerous	silly
early	noisy

Macmillan Heinemann English Language Teaching
Between Towns Road, Oxford OX4 3PP, UK

A division of Macmillan Publishers Limited

Companies and representatives throughout the world

ISBN 0 435 29356 7

First published 1997

Designed by David Brancaleone

Illustrated by: George Hollingworth, Debbie Clark, David Bowyer, Ivana Svabic, Julian Page, Ian Heard, David Brancaleone

The author would like to thank Rachel Bladon and Ranjit Rai-Quantrill for their help in the preparation and design of this book.

Printed in Thailand

2008 2007 2006 2005 2004 2003

15 14 13 12 11 10 9 8 7 6